My First
Coloring book
toddlers

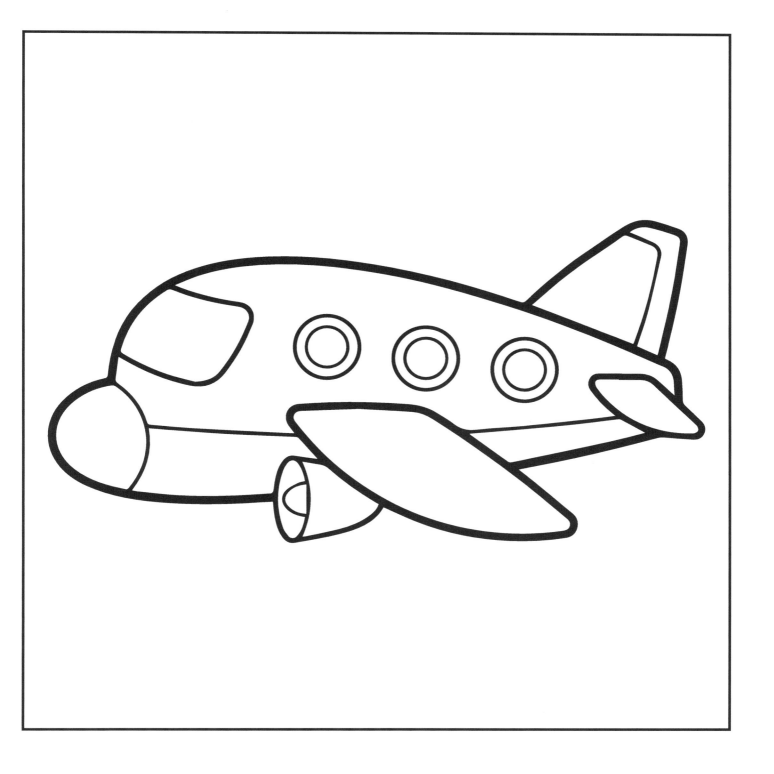

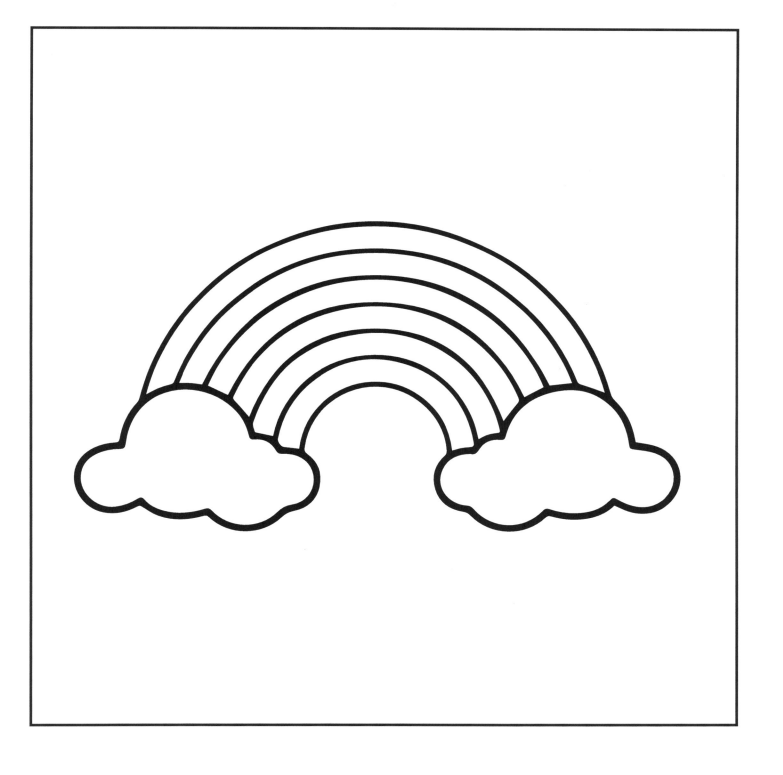

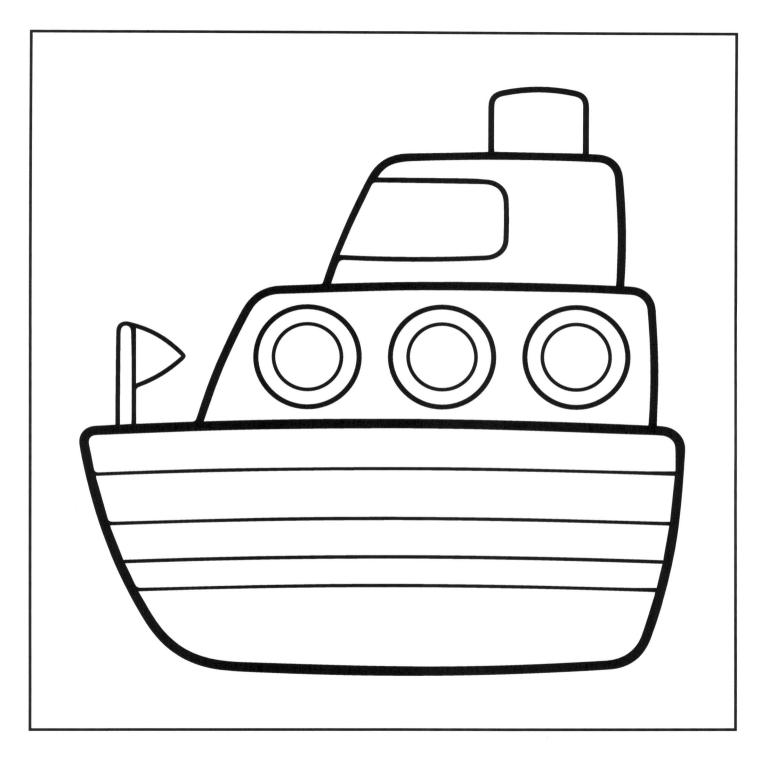

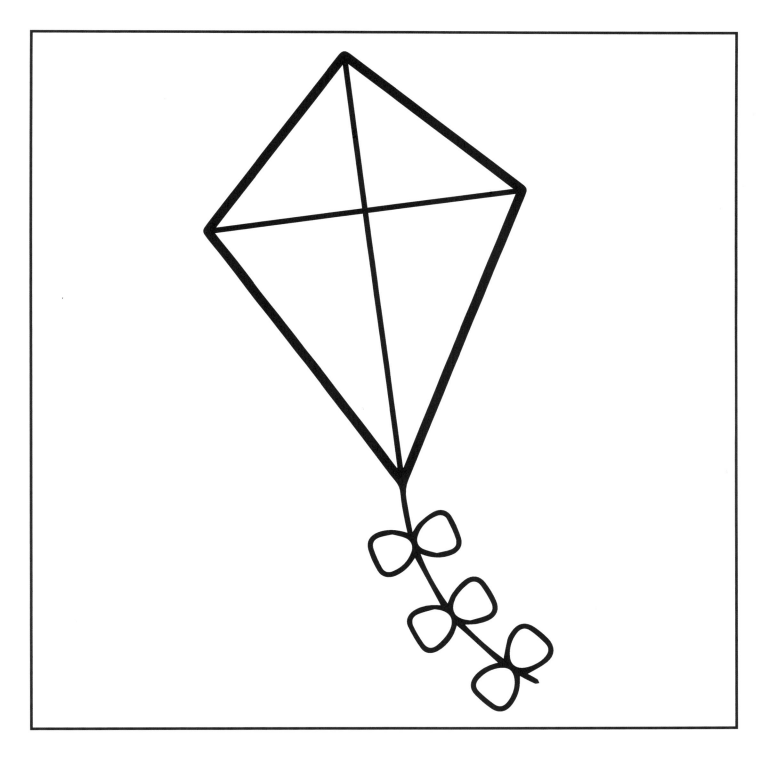

What do you think about our book?

We would be very grateful if you would leave us a review.

www.amazon.com/RYP

Go to www.amazon.com/RYP and review your recent purchases
(You can also scan the QR code with your smartphone)

Made in the USA
Coppell, TX
06 December 2024

41779816R10031